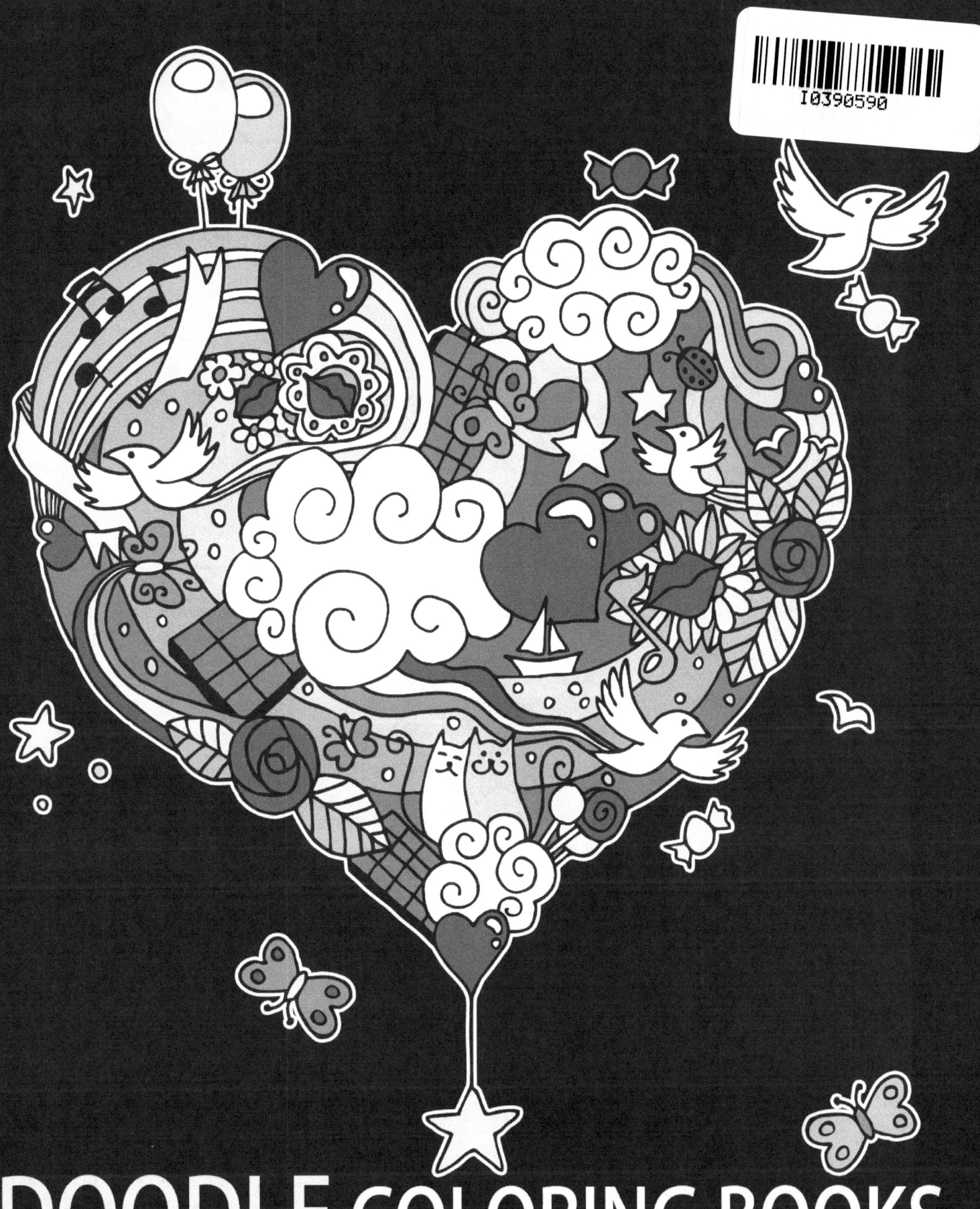

DOODLE COLORING BOOKS

Stress Relieving Flower, Animal
and Doodle Designs

TEST YOUR COLOR

TEST YOUR COLOR

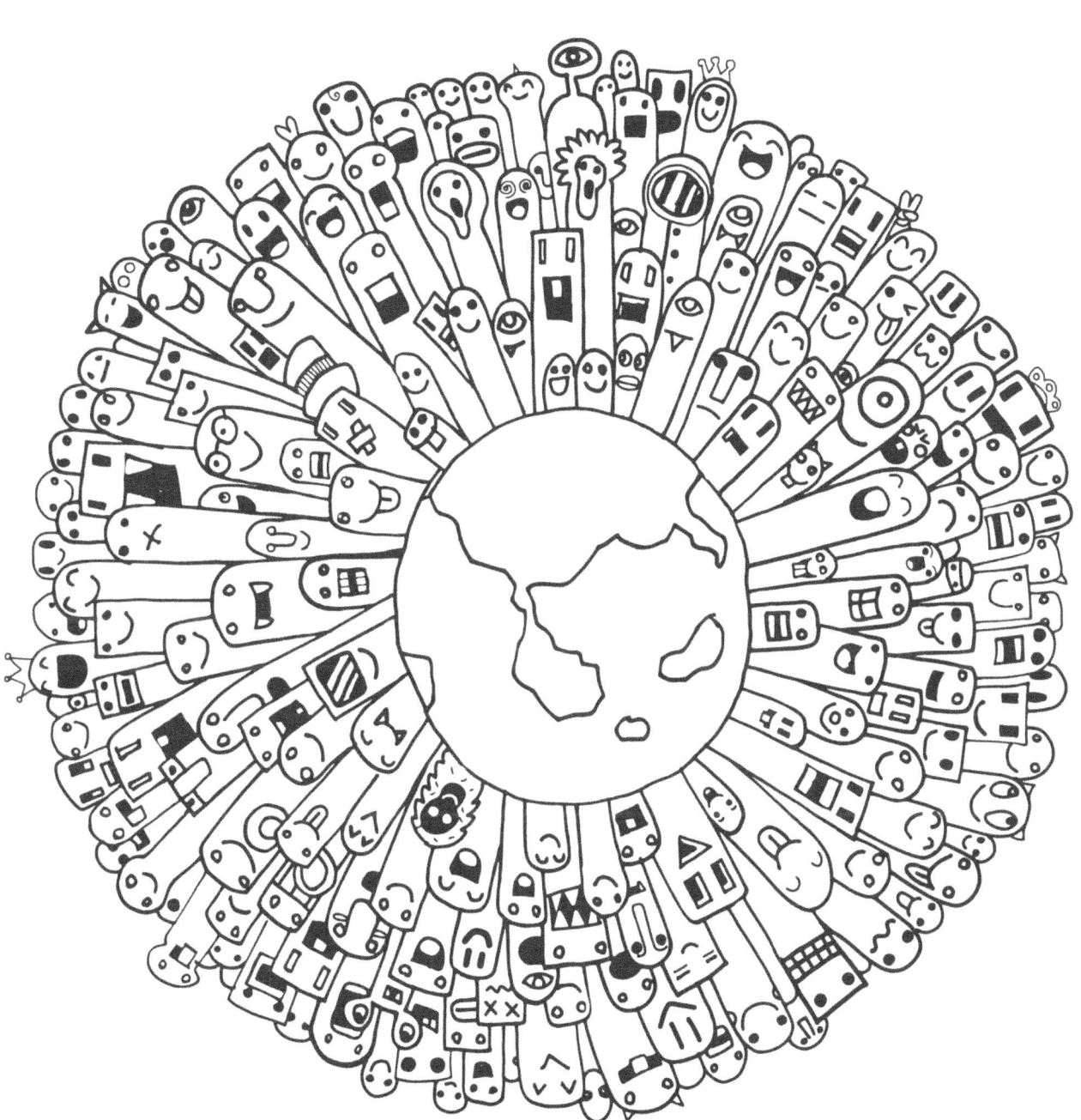

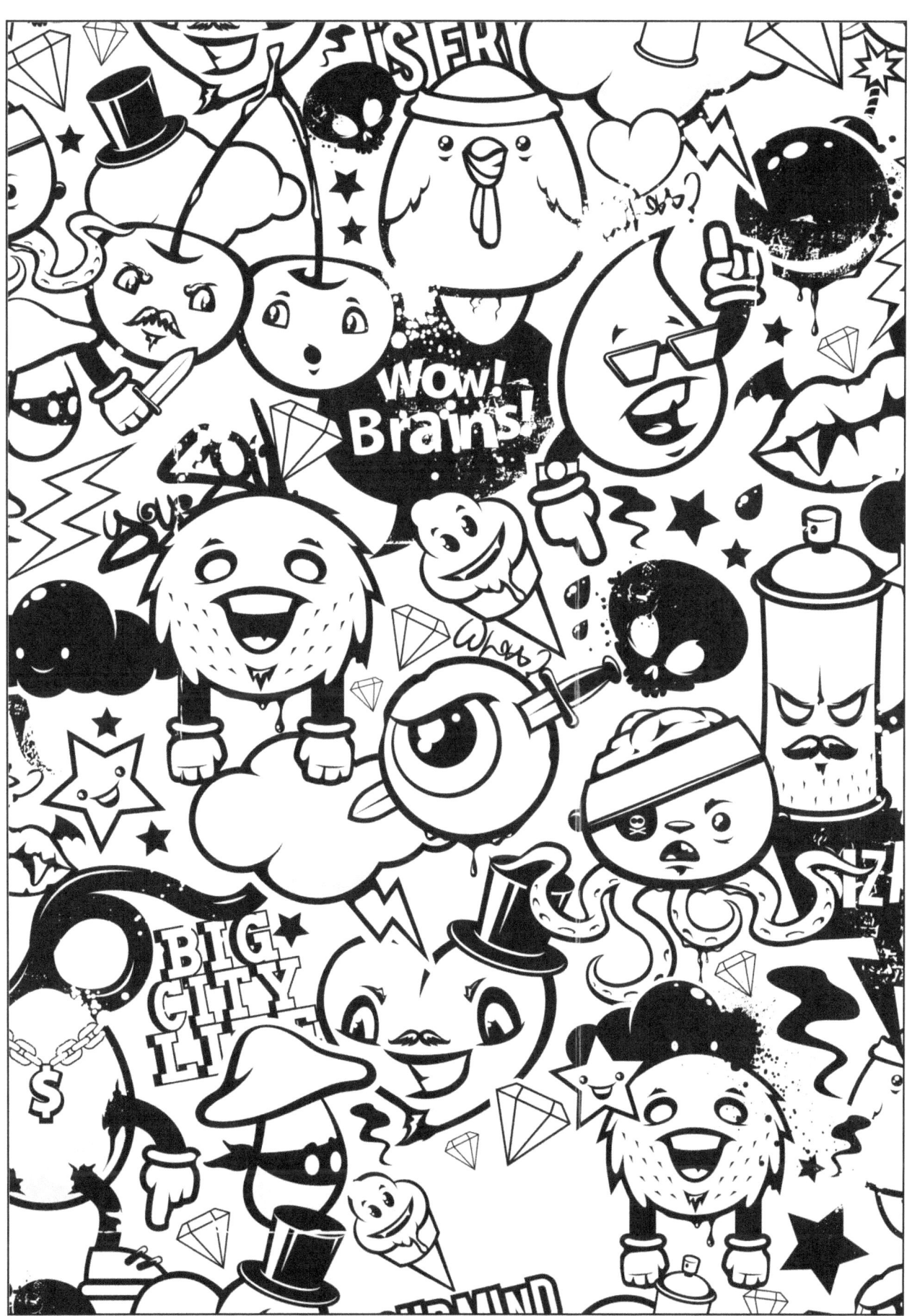

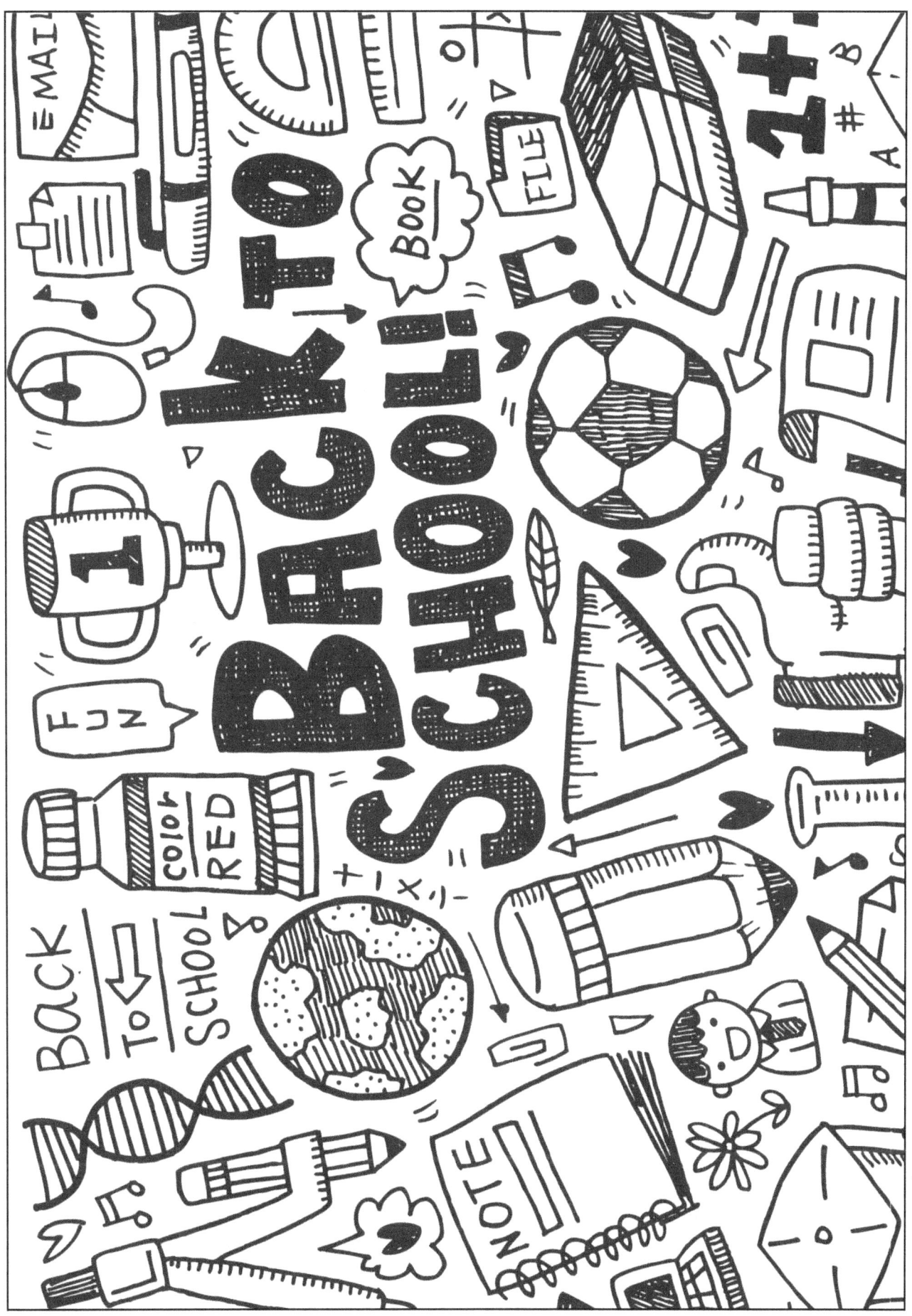

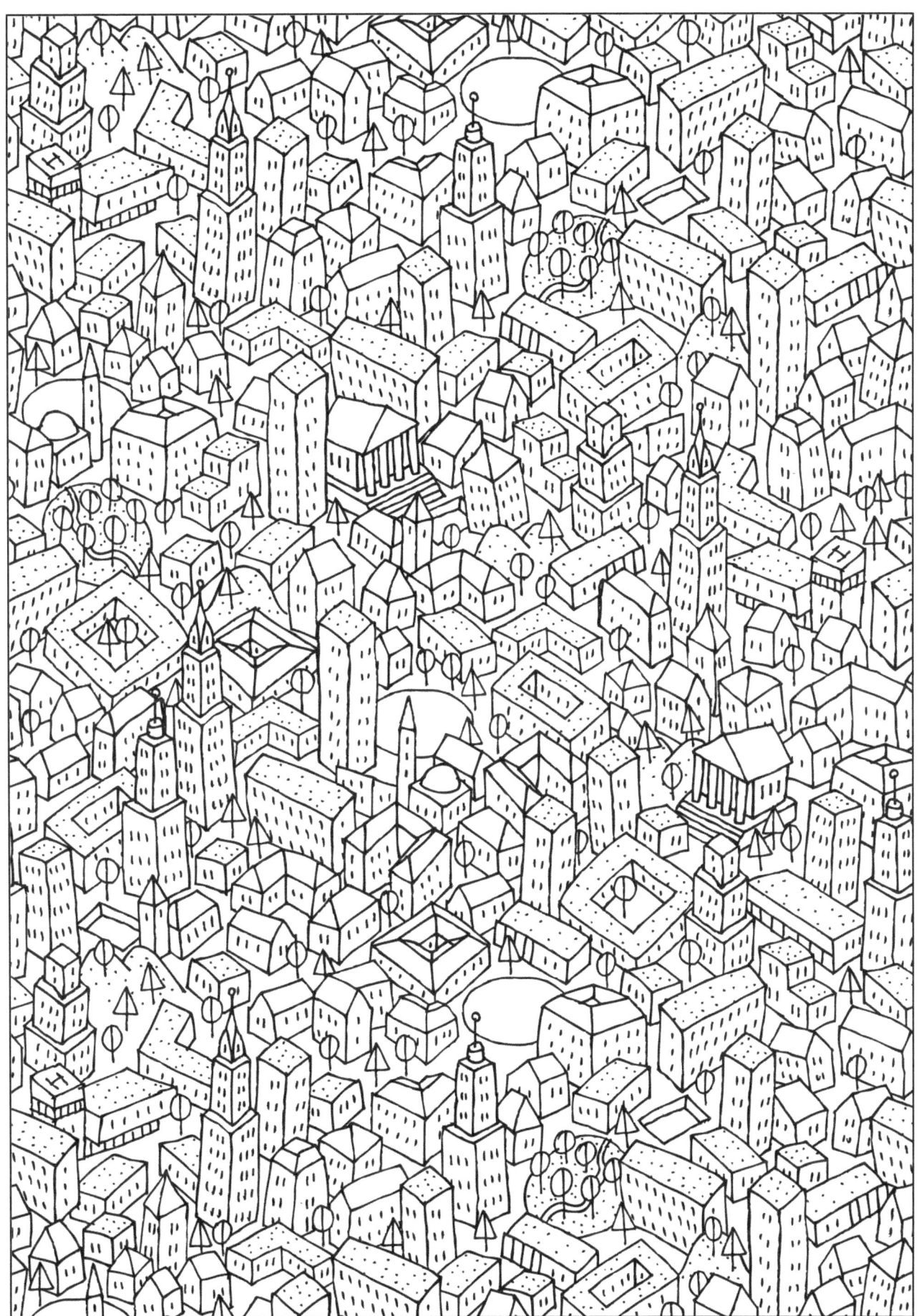

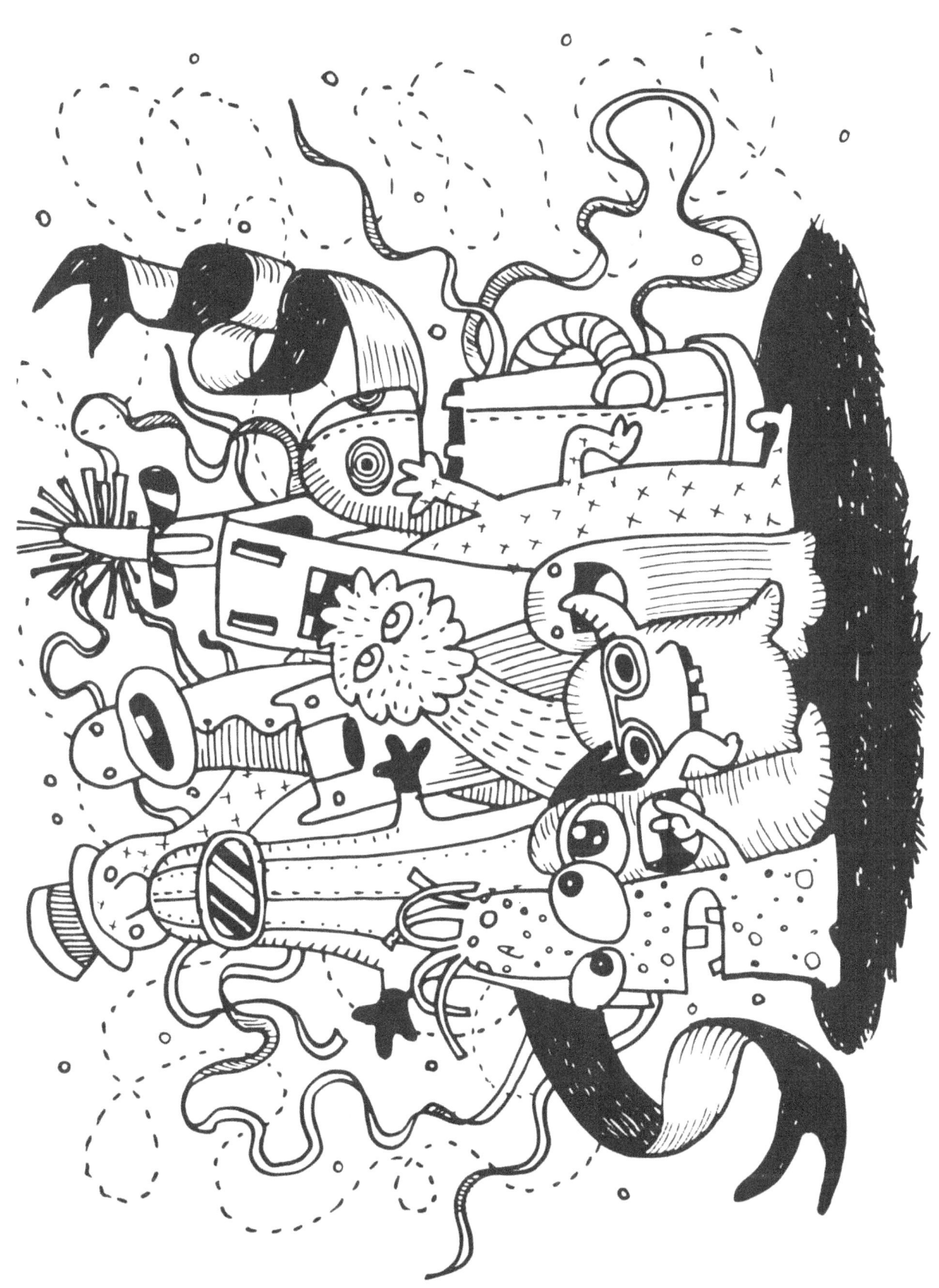

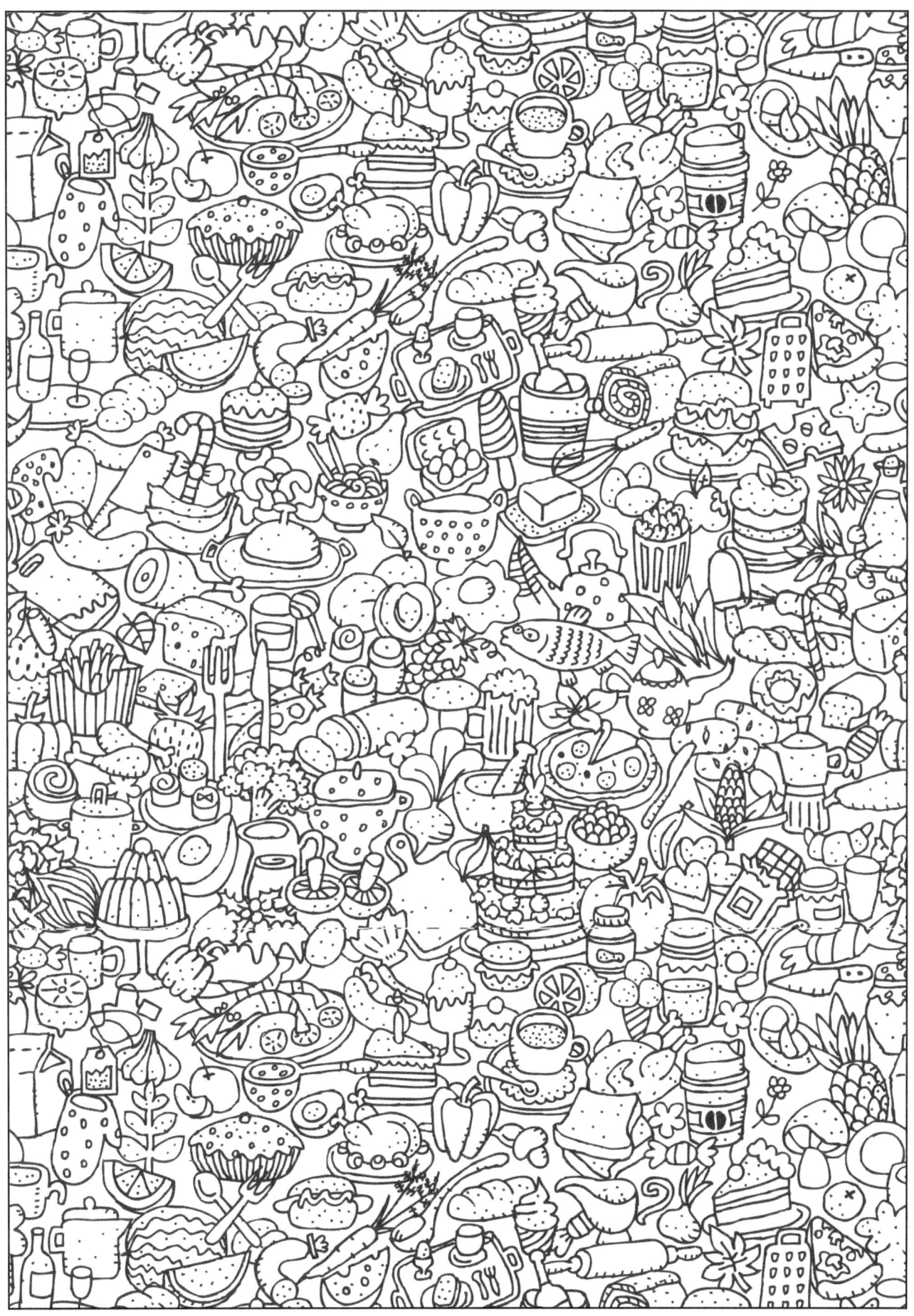

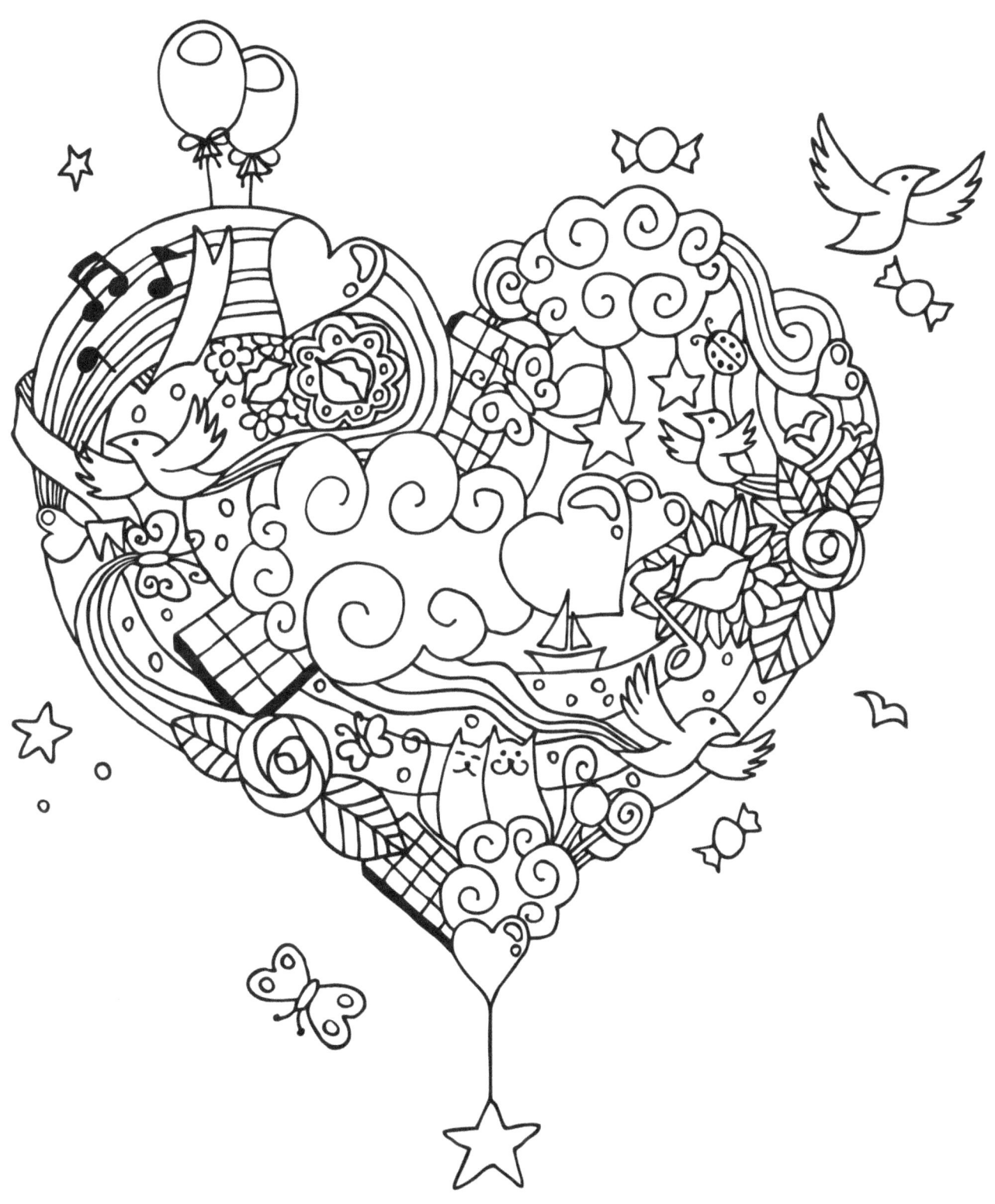

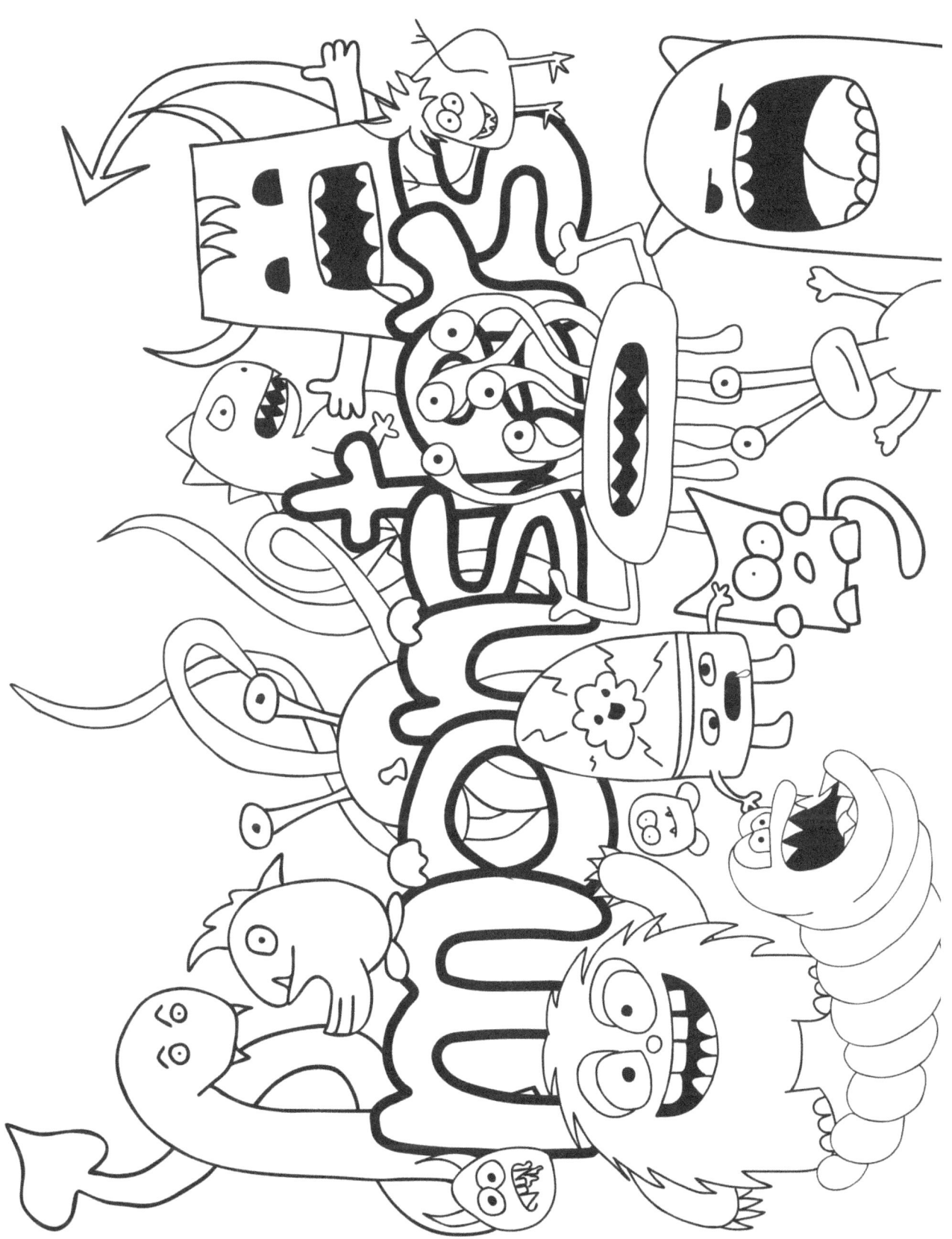

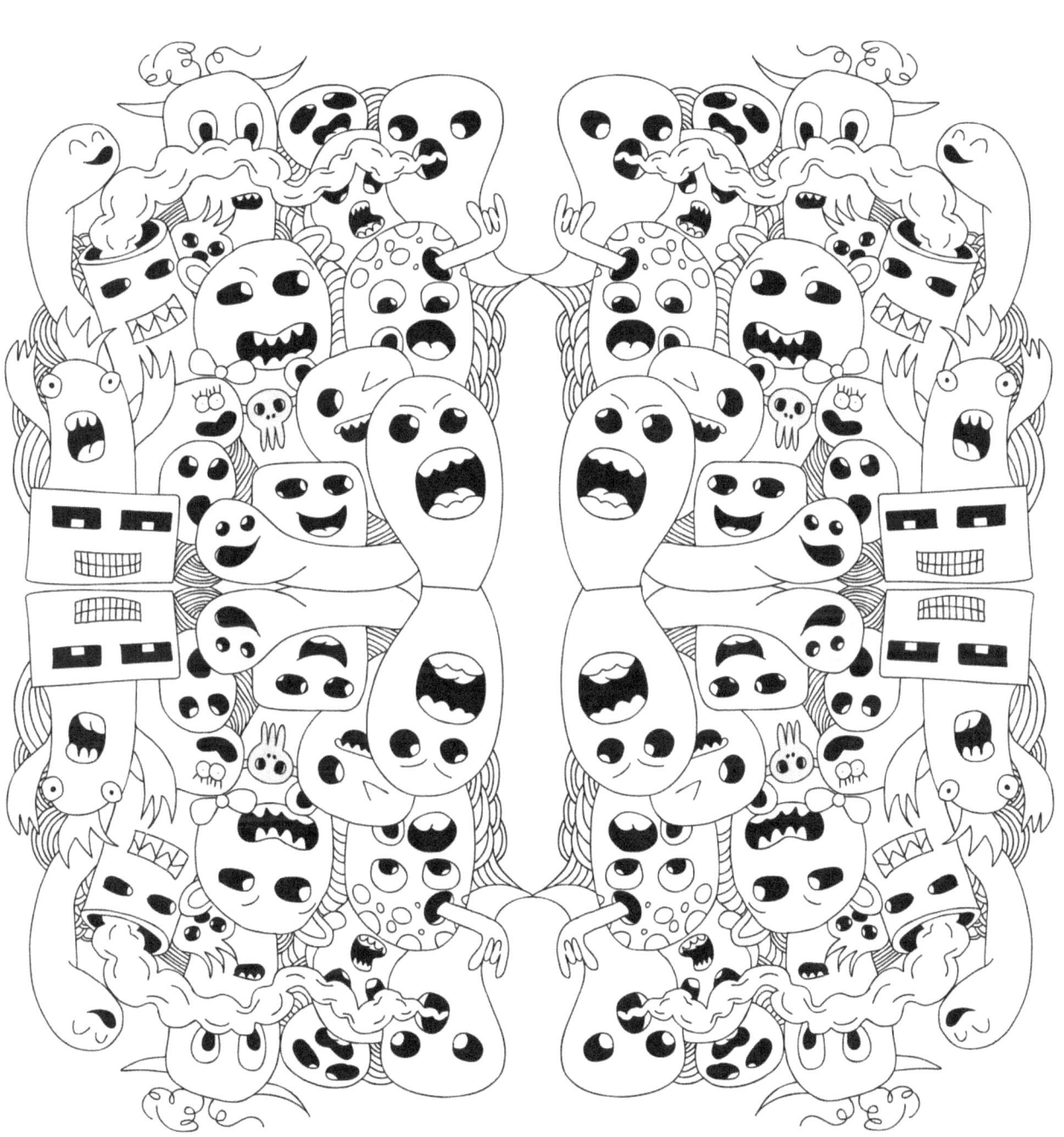

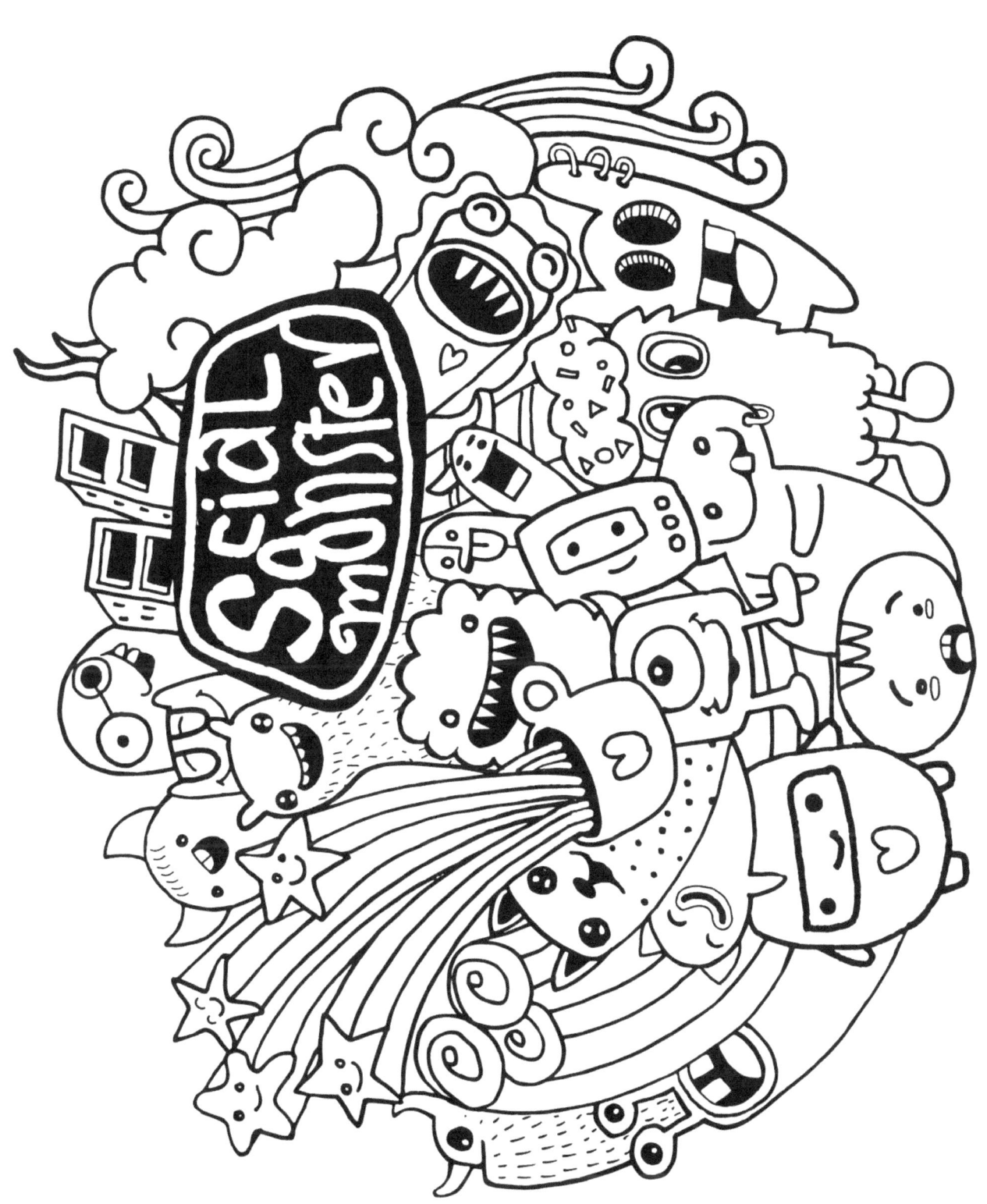

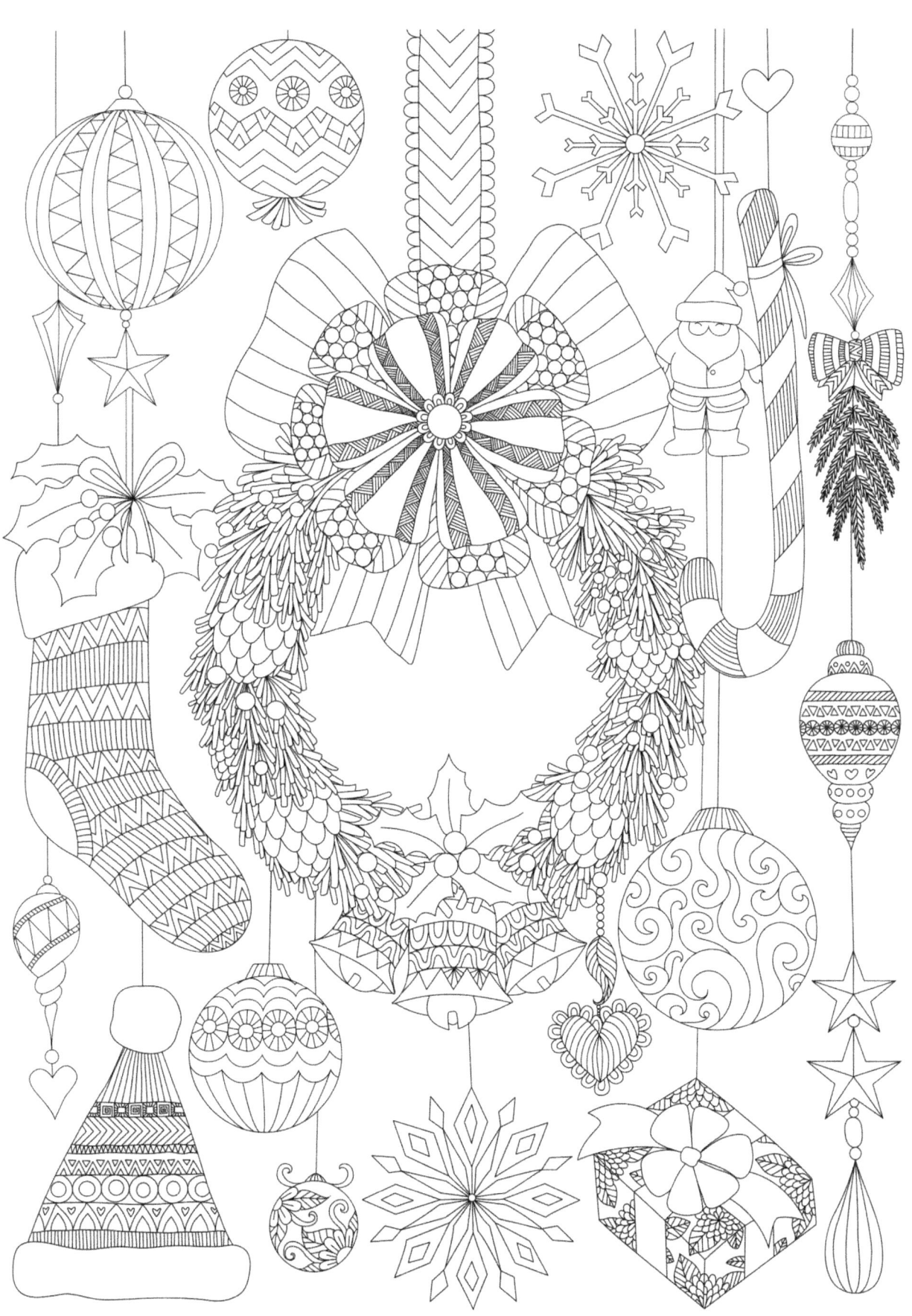

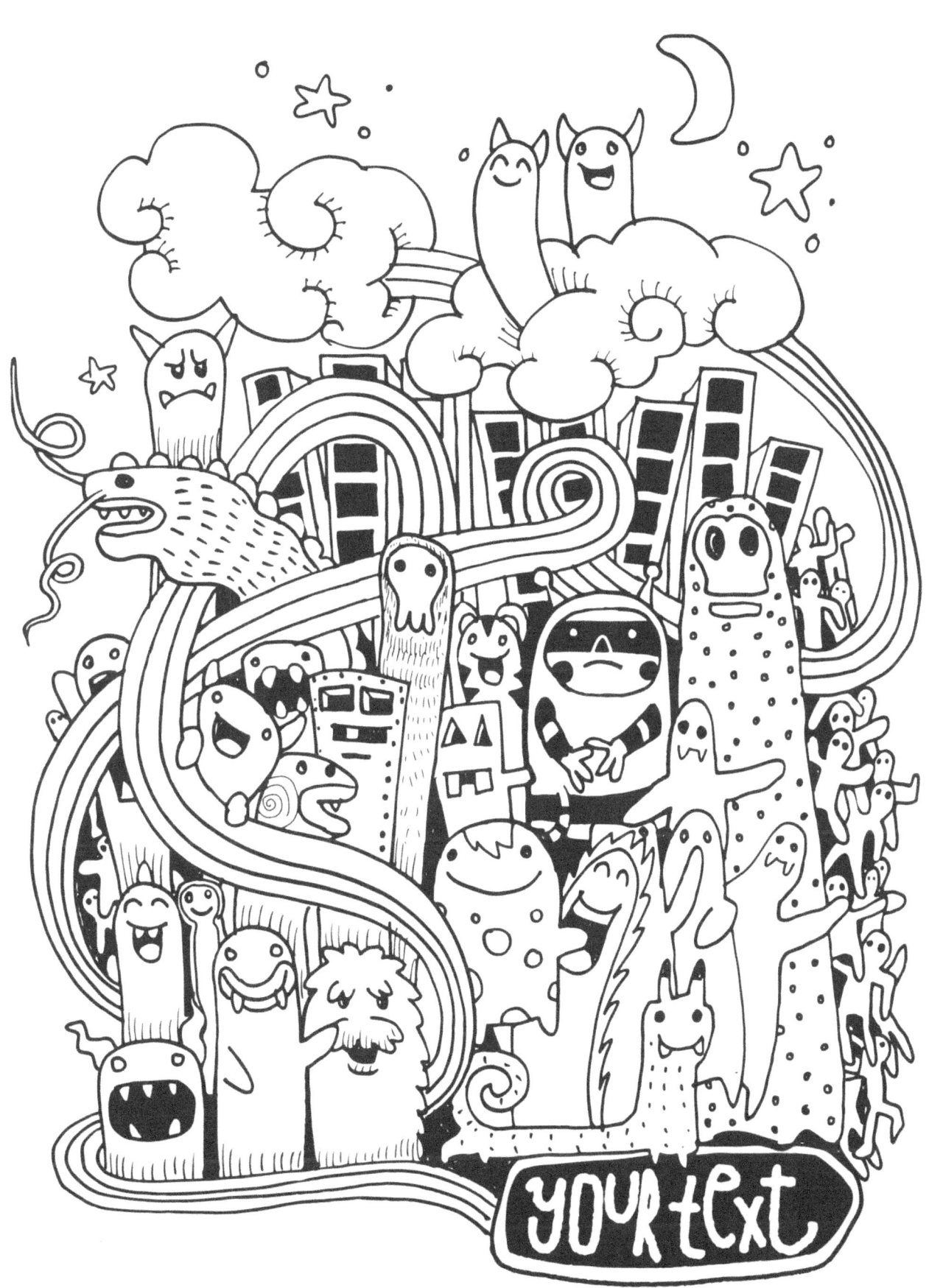

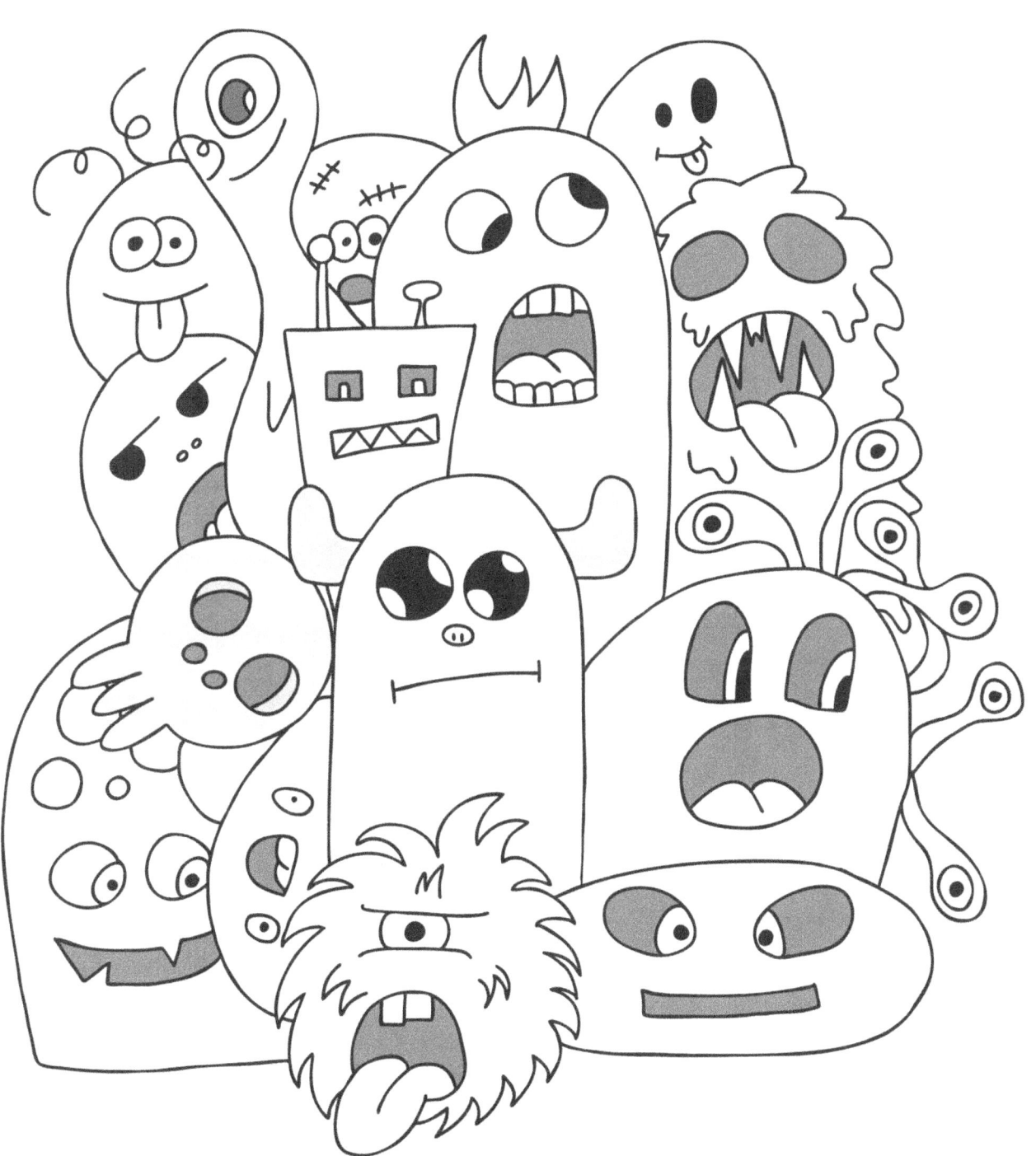

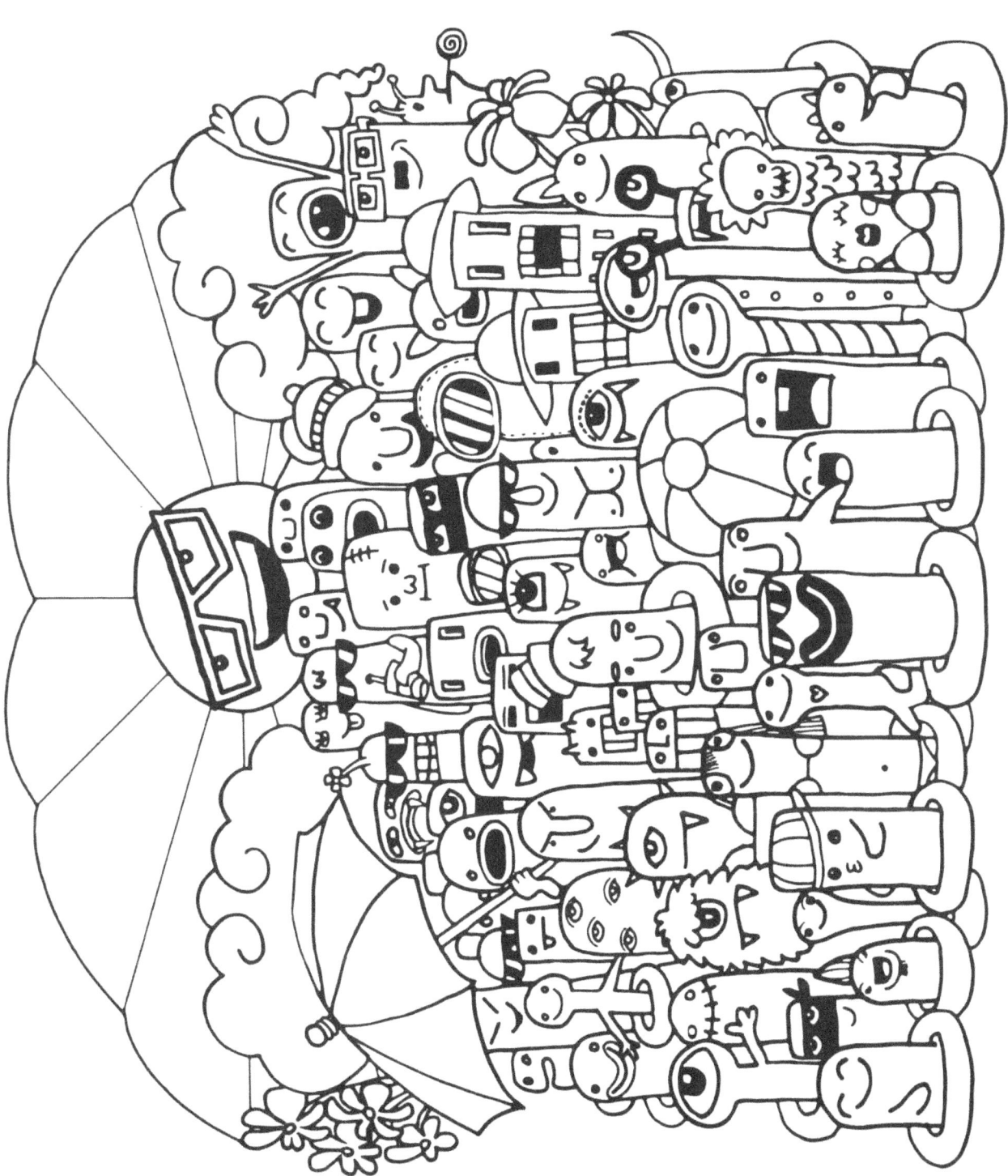

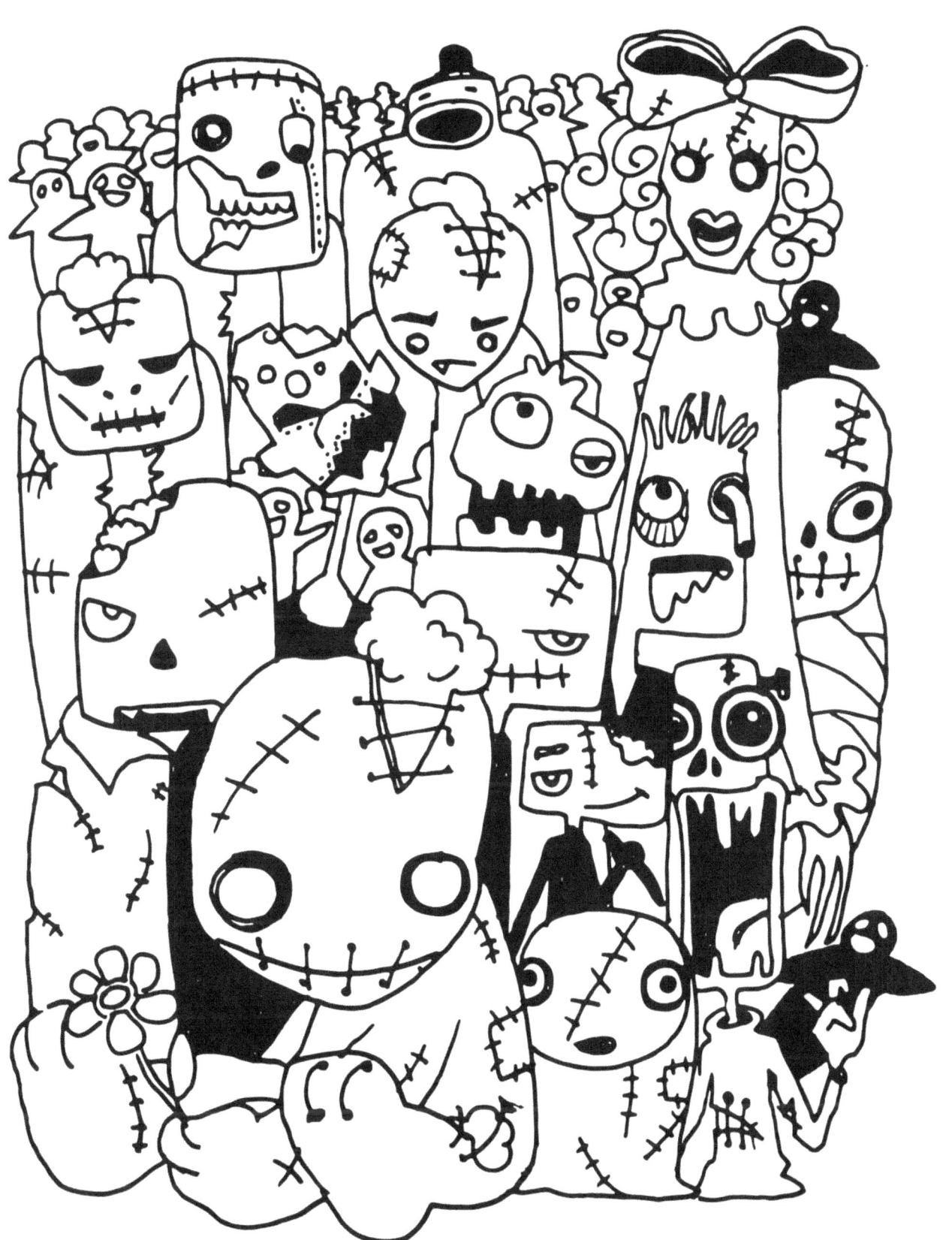

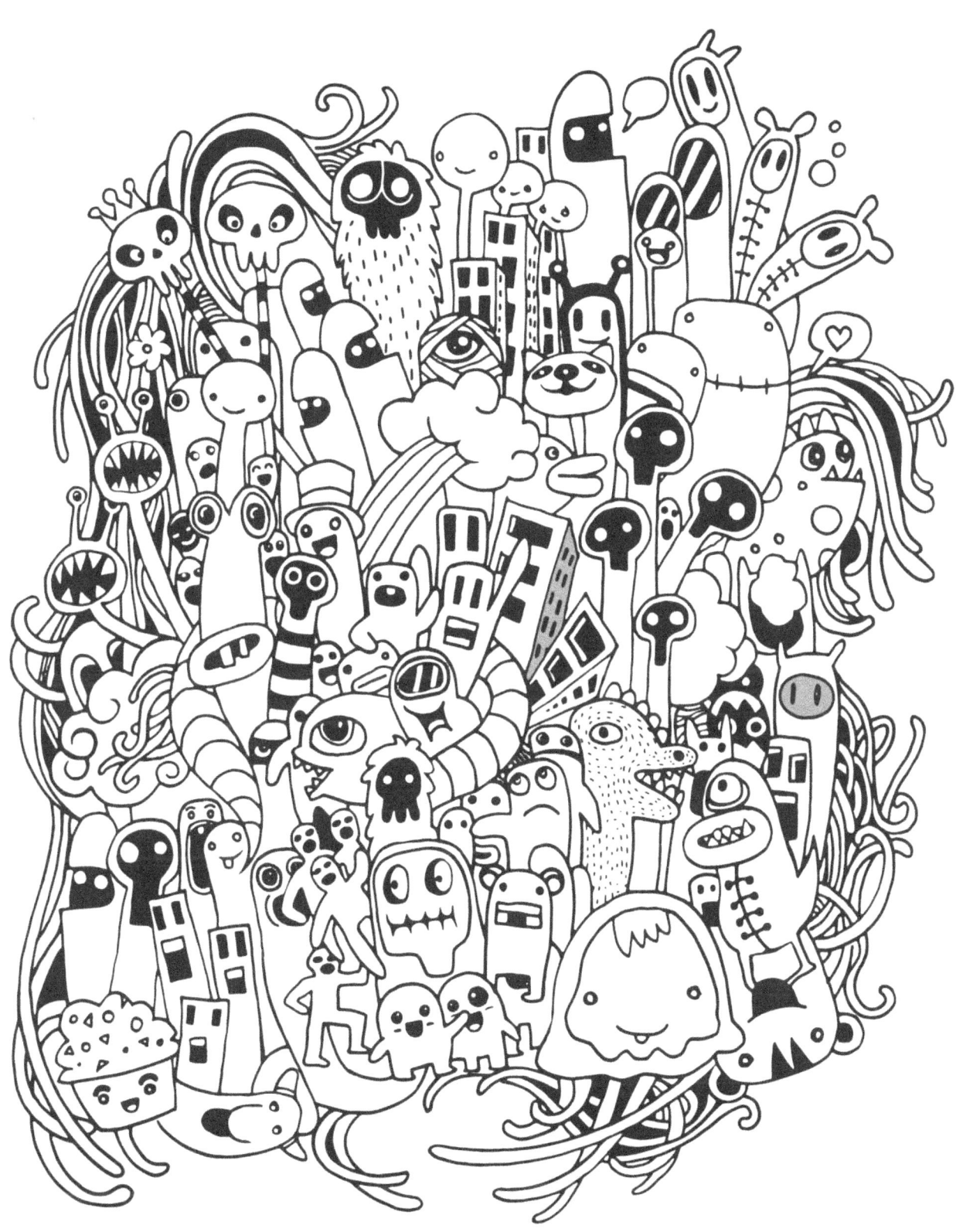

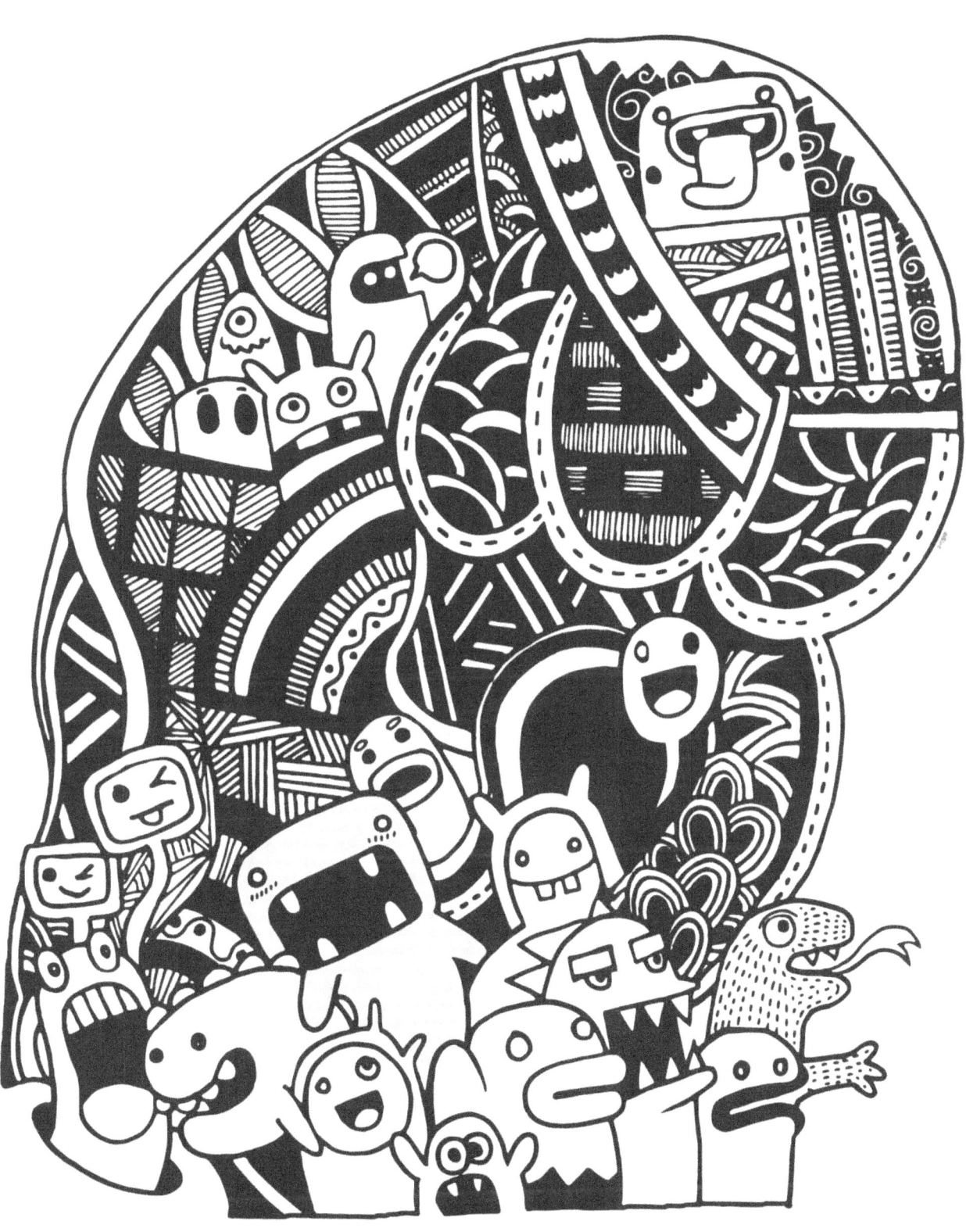

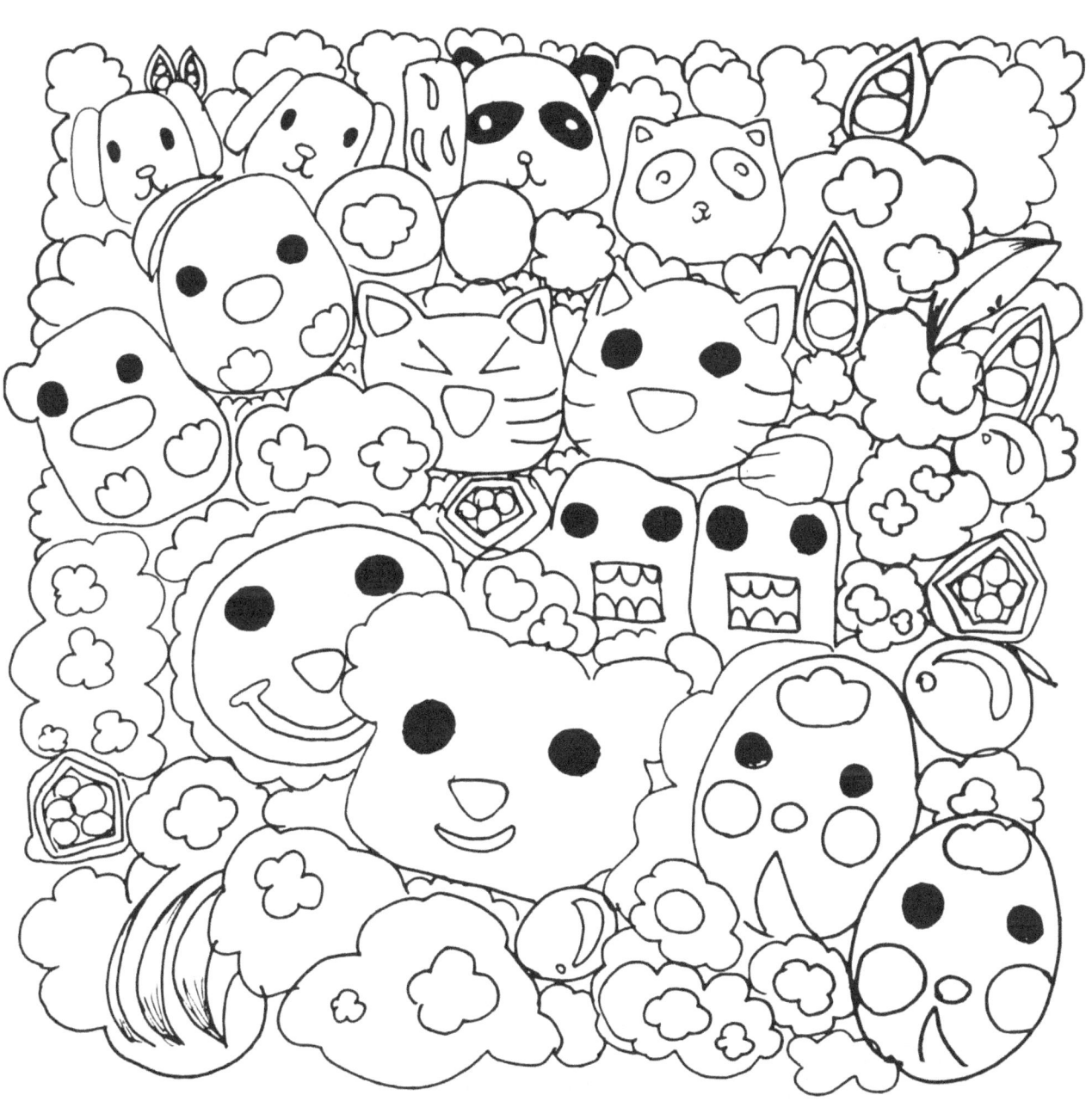

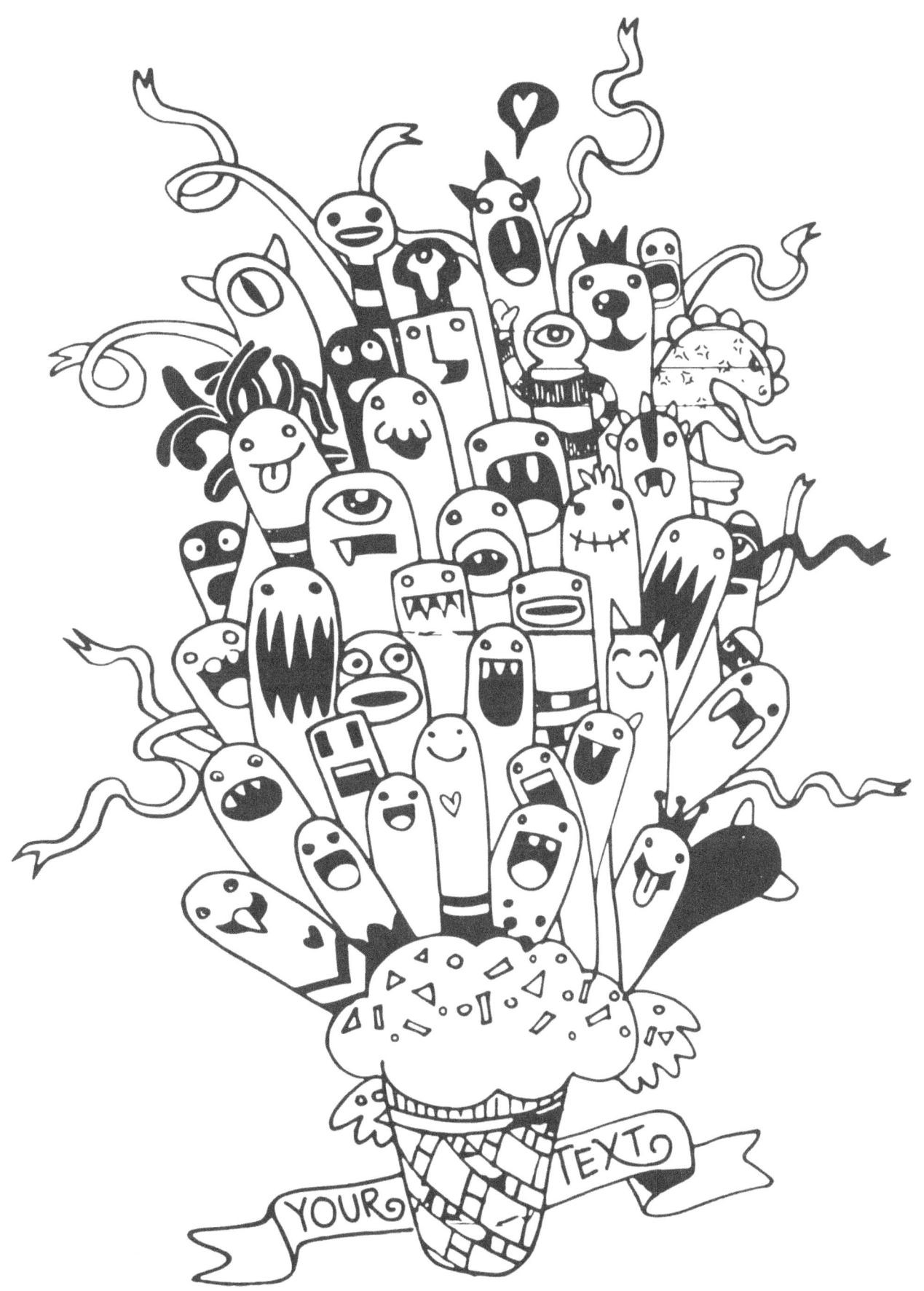

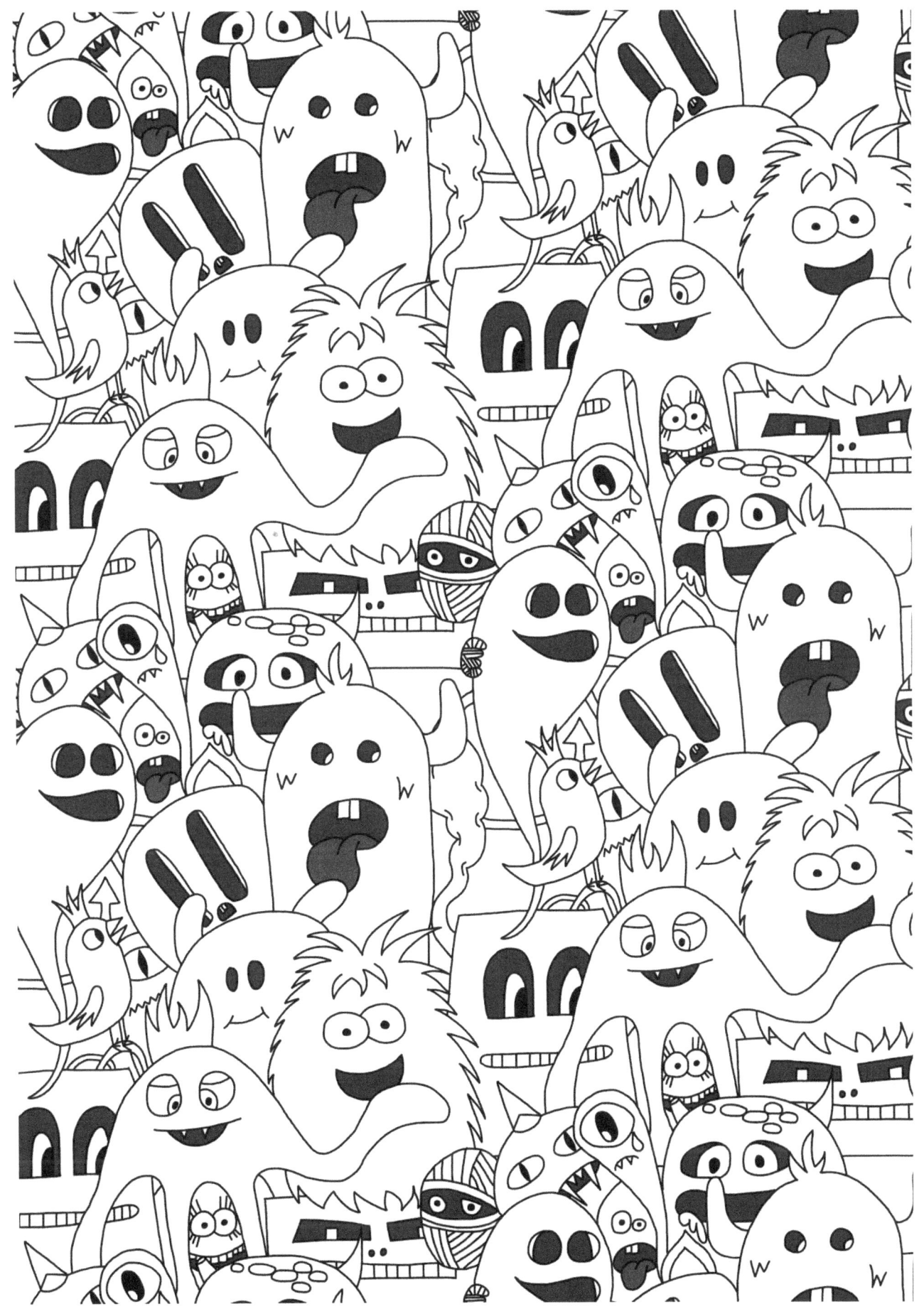

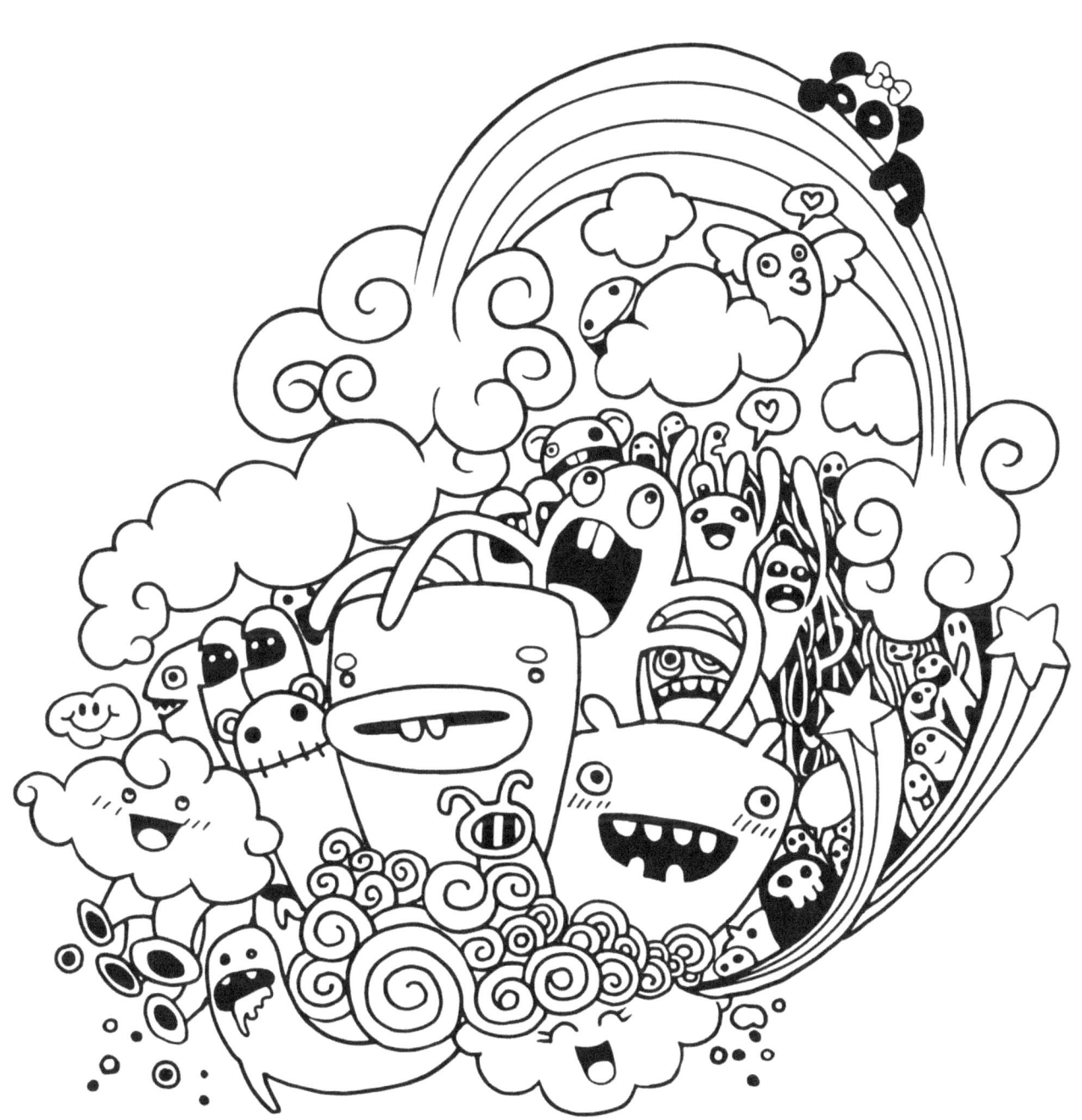

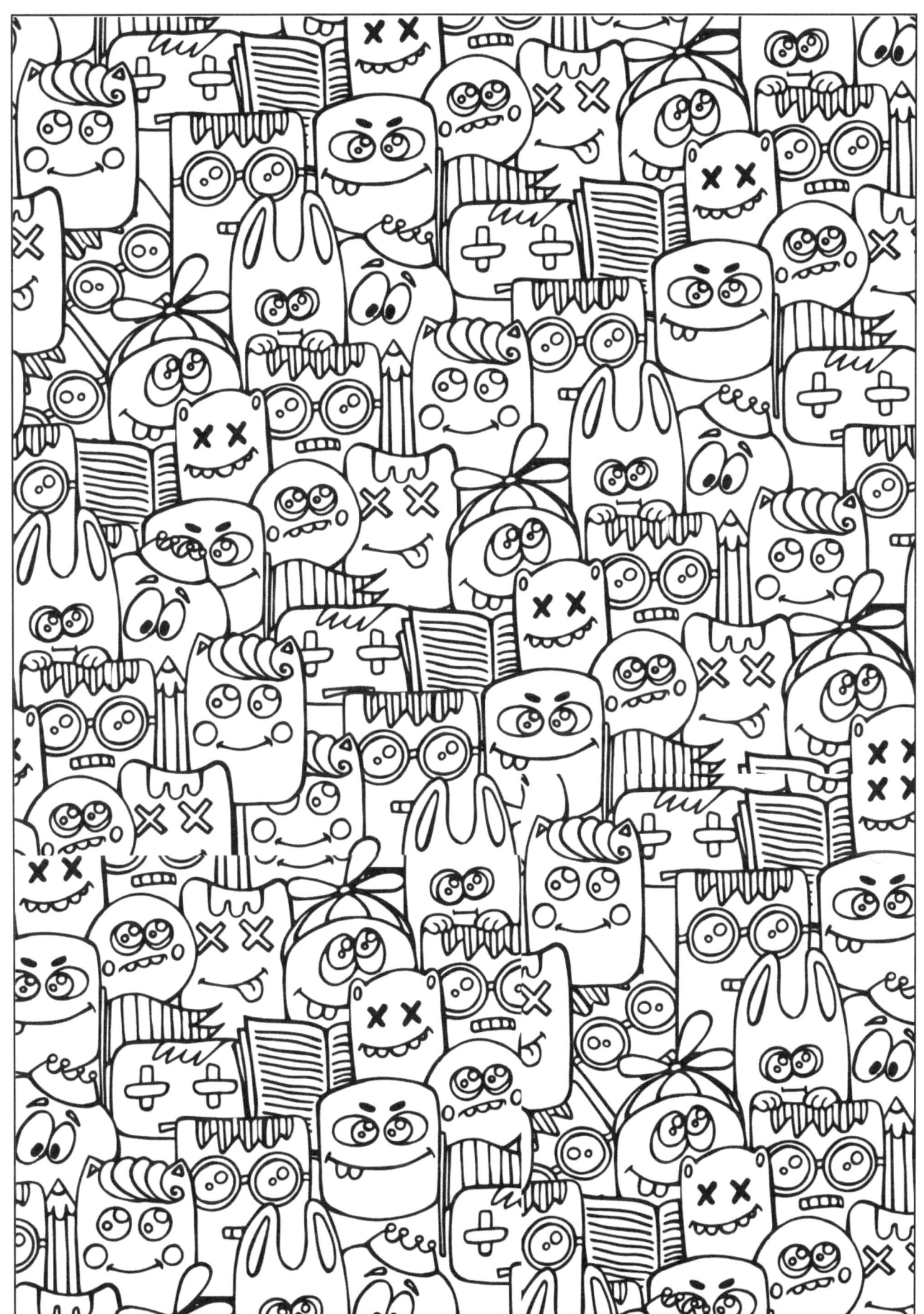

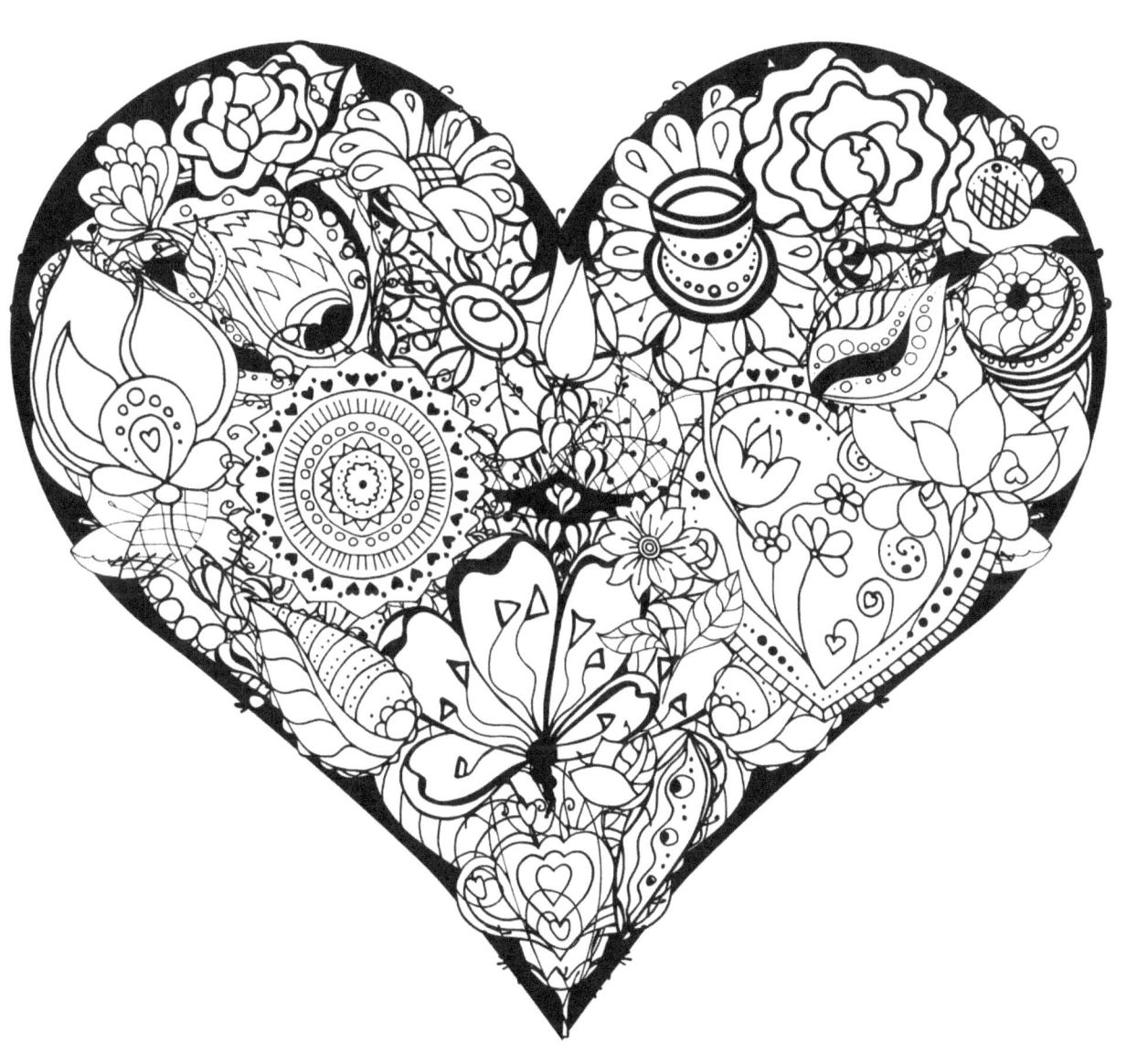

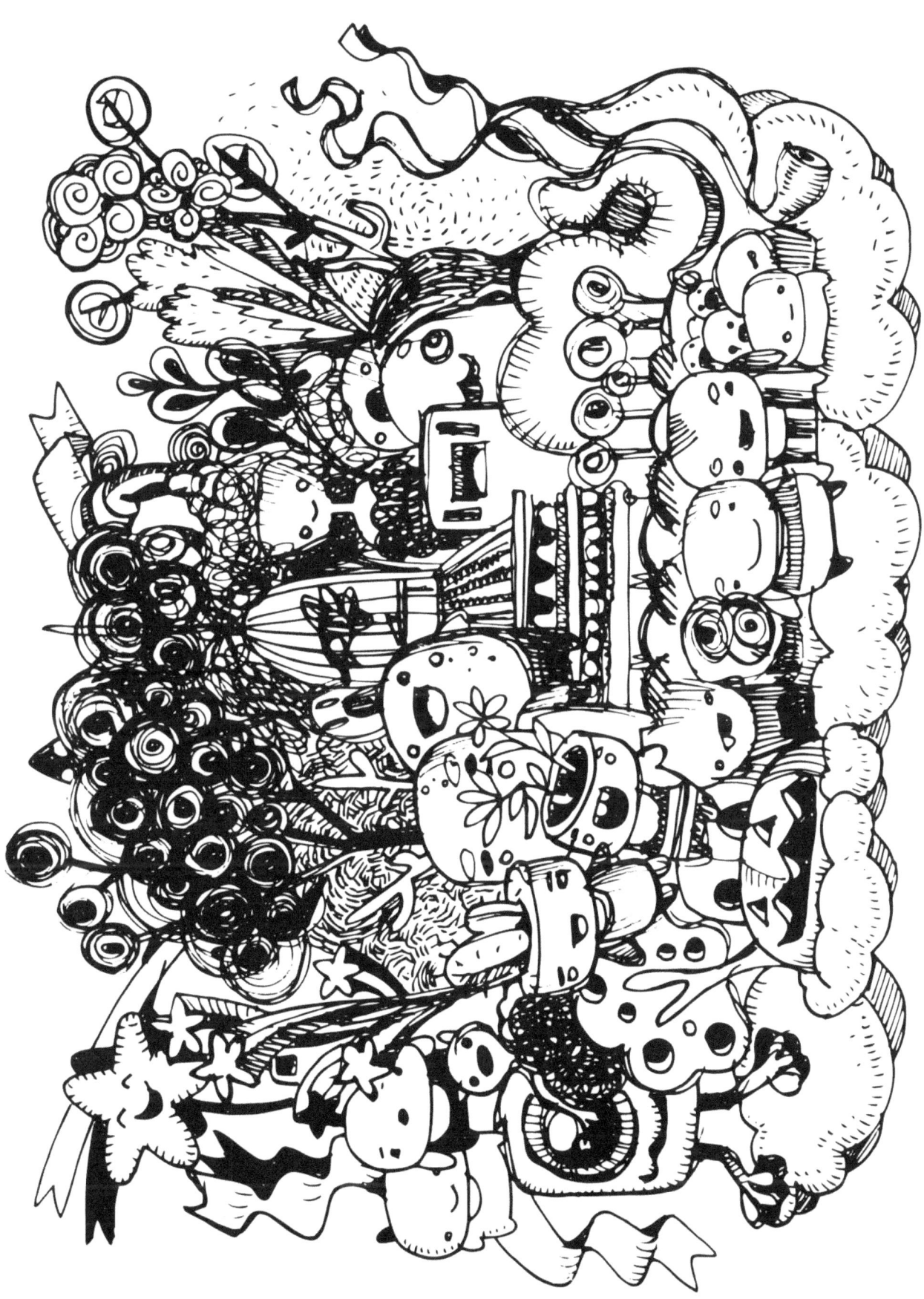

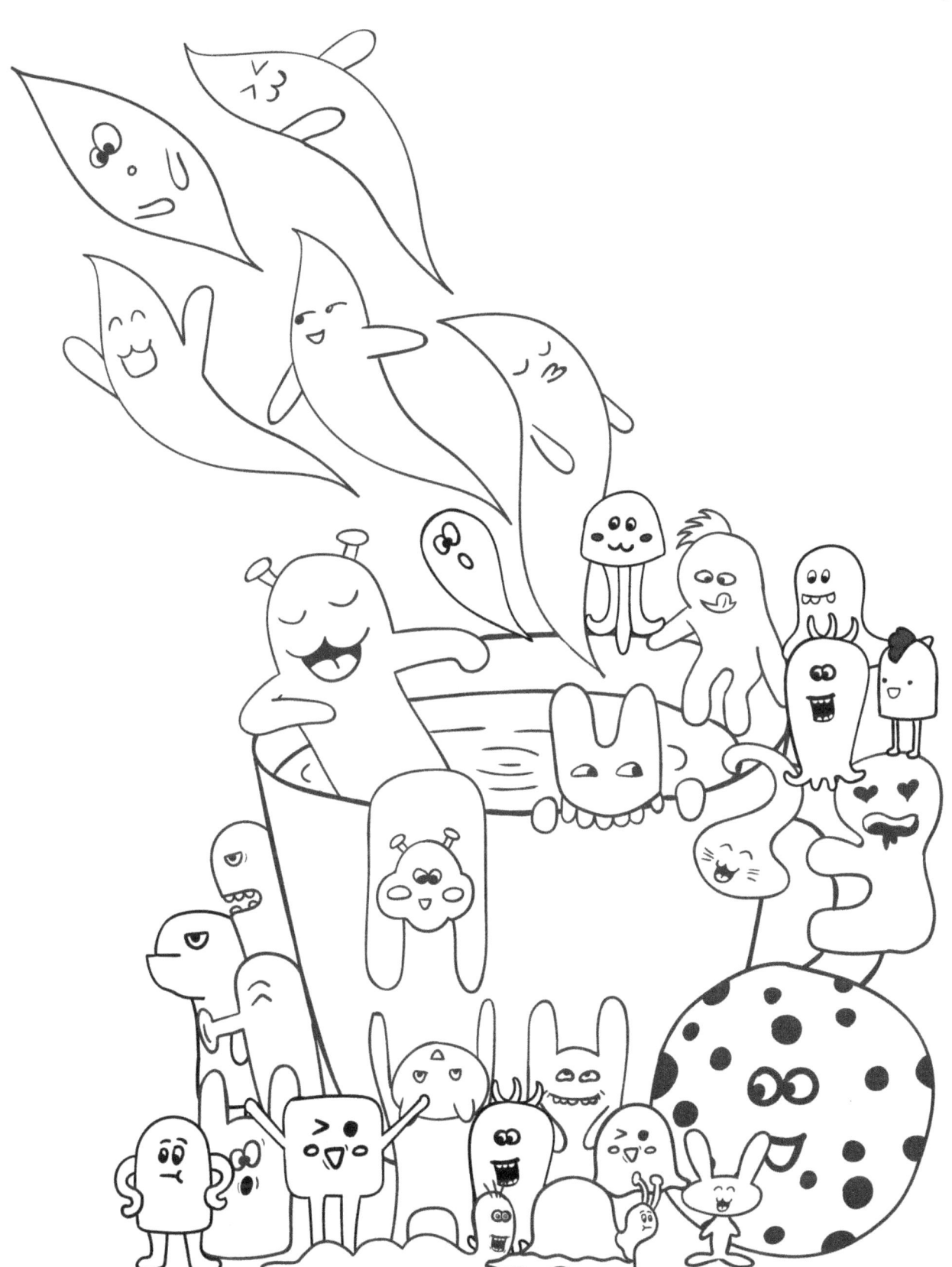

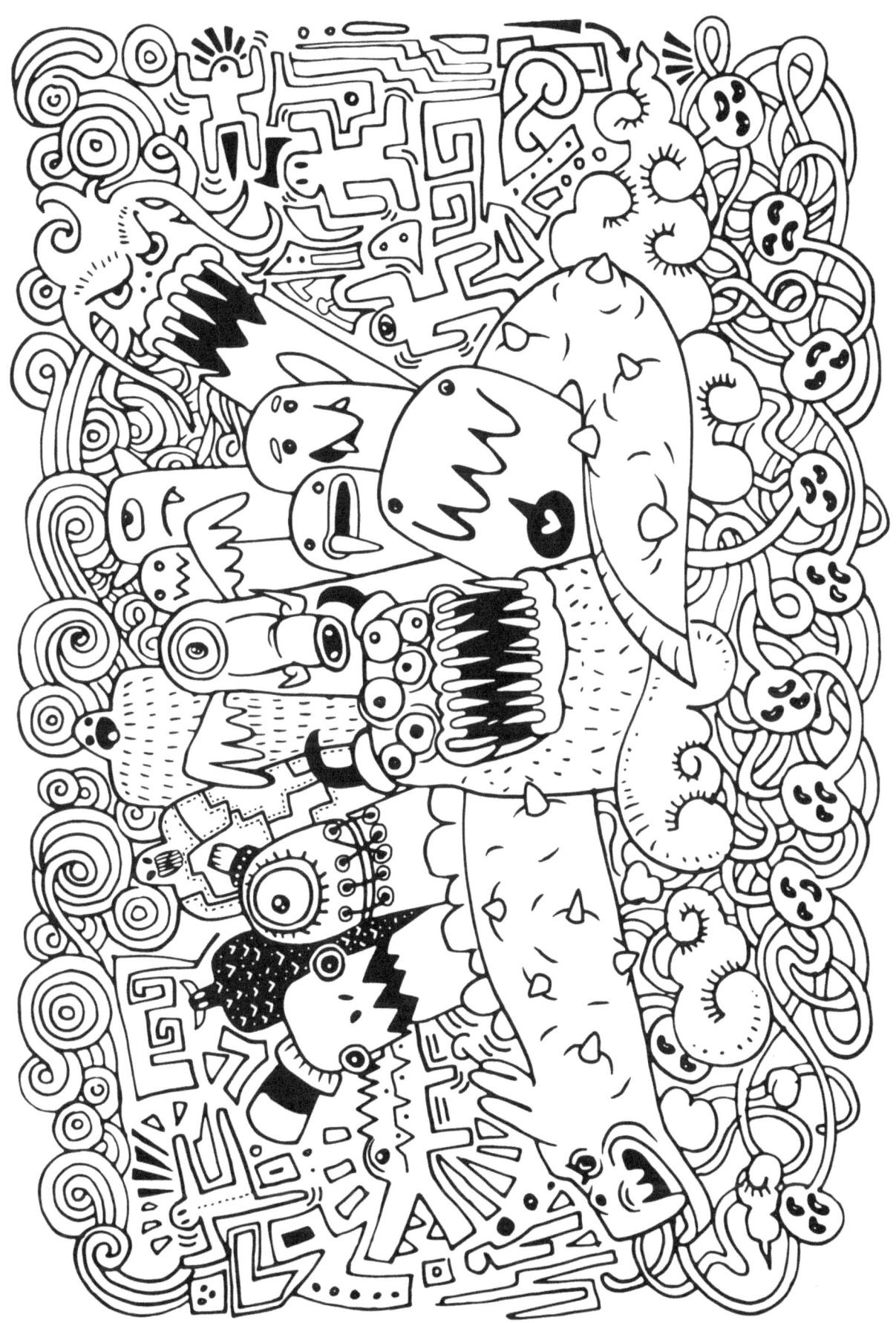

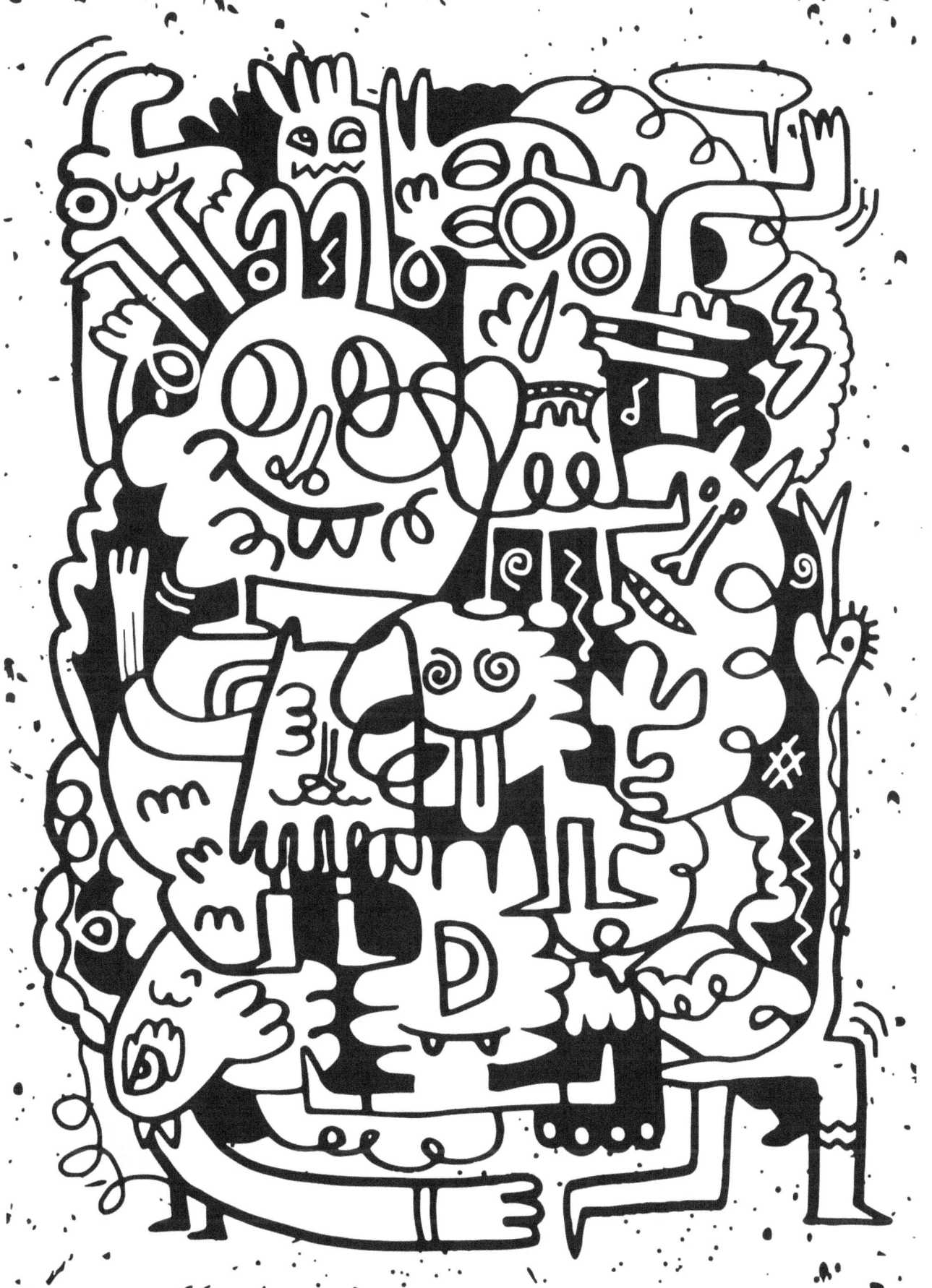

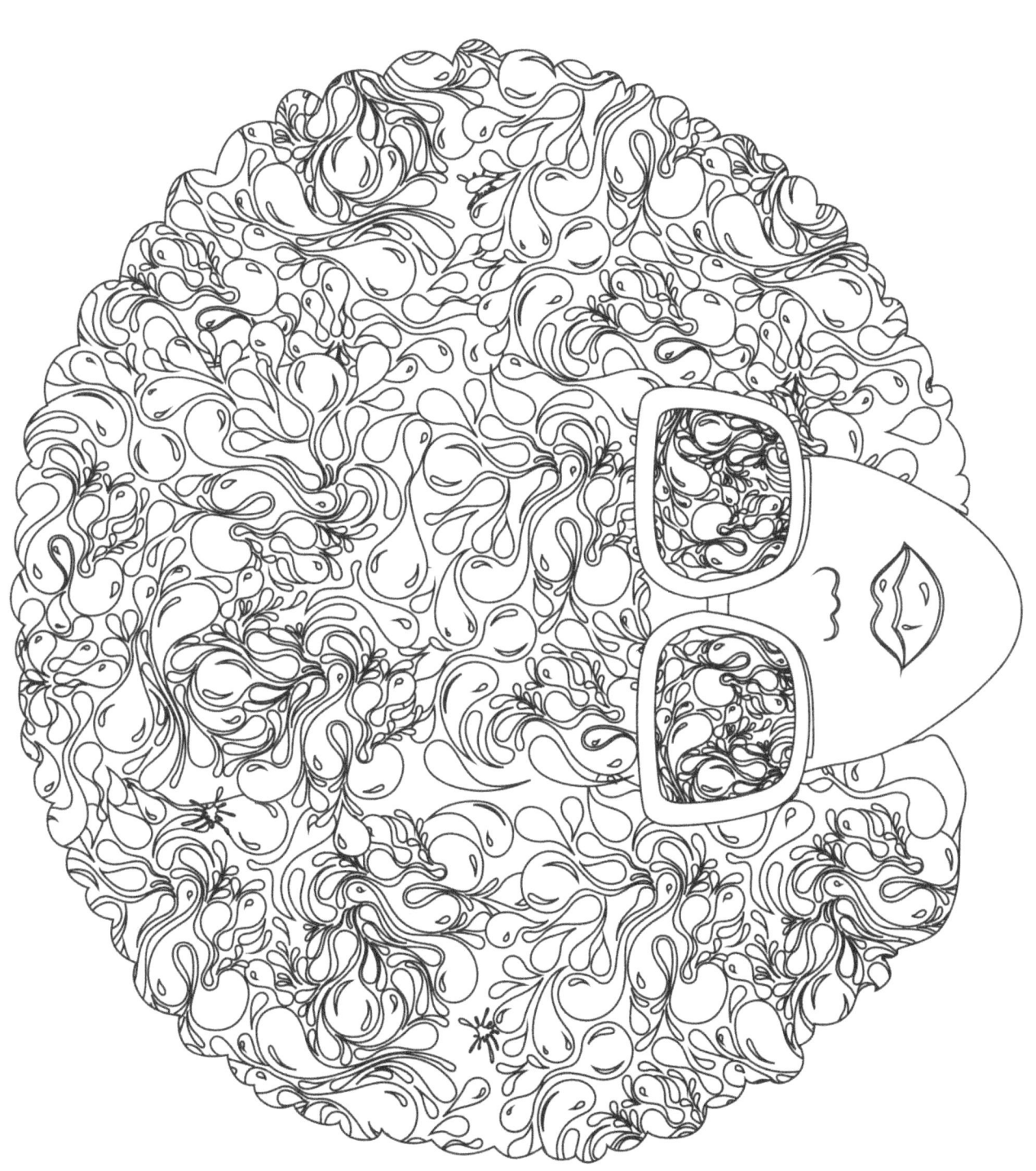

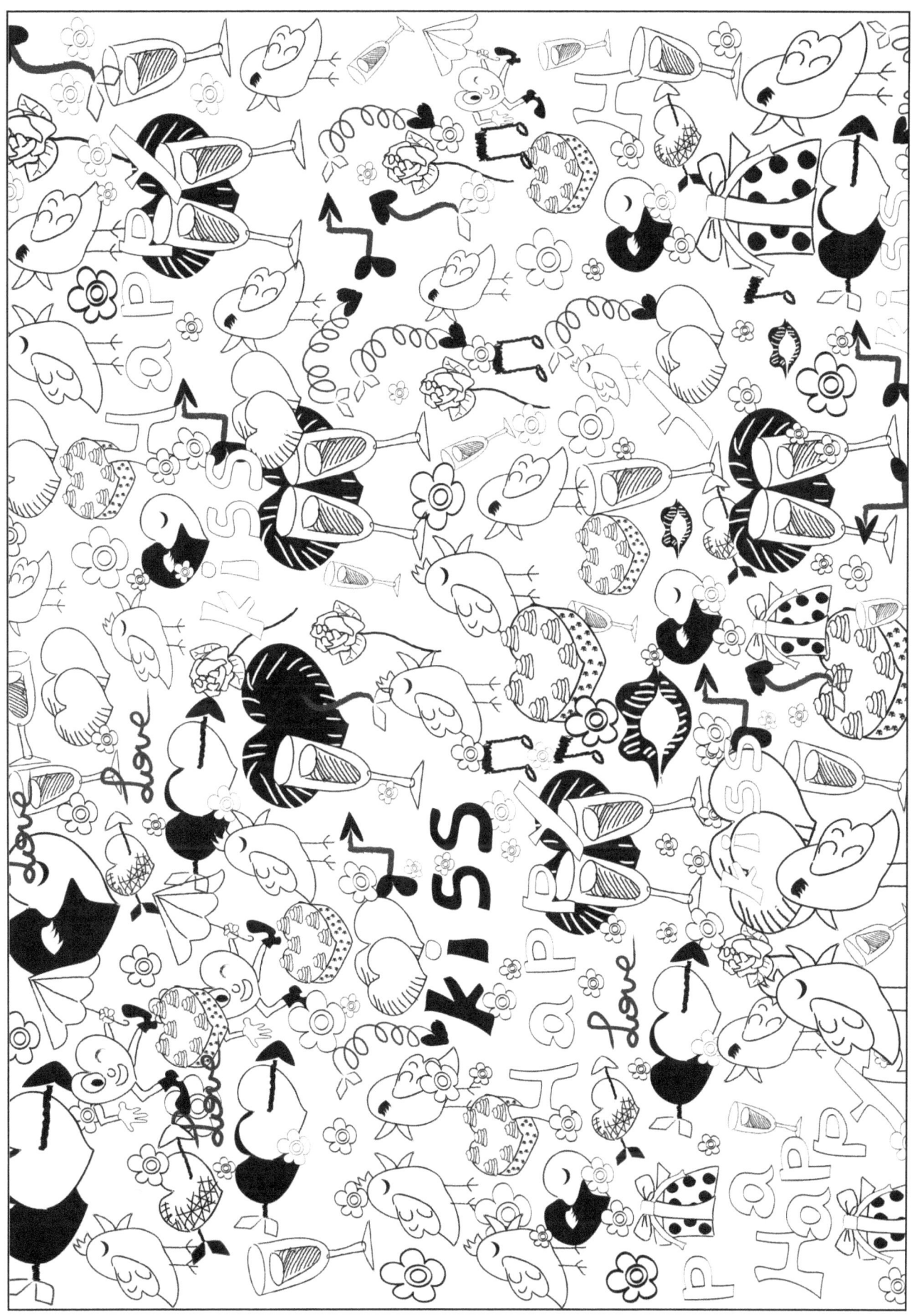

www.ingramcontent.com/pod-product-compliance
Lightning Source LLC
Chambersburg PA
CBHW081255180526
45170CB00007B/2441